The Hustle Code

Detroit King Tape

THE HUSTLE CODE

Change your perceptions
Change your circumstances
with
Empowering codes
written by
DETROIT KING TAPE

Book Cover by Myles Kessler

1st edition 2024

Print: 979-8-9908780-0-6

Ebook: 979-8-9908780-1-3

Hardcover: 979-8-9908780-2-0

I would like to thank the creator For guiding me on this path. Plus allowing me to learn the necessary information through my experiences, which brought this book into existence. Special thanks to Andre "Bear" White and everyone who participated in making this project a reality. Thx to all supportive family, loved ones and friends. Again, Most importantly Thanks to the Creator, for giving me the light, plus guidance to persevere through obstacles that would have broken many. I will forever be grateful as I continue to manifest greatness on this journey of "Health-n-Hustle".

Salute to all the hustler's making it happen, to all the hustler's who fell short, and to all of the hustlers who gave their lives trying to feed their families and chase their dreams. R.I.H.

Contents

Introduction

Two things you must have in life: health and hustle. Not having both is like buying a new car without wheels or flying a wingless airplane - YOU'RE STUCK! You become grounded with limited choices, from reaching your goals and being stranded in a dead-end job, to unbalanced relationships, and low self-esteem.

HUMBLE IN THE JUNGLE

Forget what you heard; you'll get eaten alive even in everyday life if you don't have a hustler's mentality. Walked-on. Passed by. Looked over. Pushed and shoved into a box, labeled as insignificant. Sounds familiar?

The Hustle Code can show you how to master advantageous moves. How to change a flat life with a highflying attitude. How to get credit for your ideas. How to not be a stunt double for a turn. How to put yourself in the mindset of not accepting second best. *Hustlers don't wait to get chosen!*

They present the options and select the best outcome.

These hustle codes are designed for people who want to

maximize their position and take it to another level.

The Hustle Code is the blueprint to change circumstances, perceptions, and redirect energy for your prerogative. Anything in demand inherits a hustle. You have a product, idea or self-image – whatever it is – The Hustle Code provides references and real-life examples on how to turn a negative into a positive outcome. This book isn't about losing or winning, failure or success. Though its contents can be used to achieve favorable ends, the intent is to bring out your inner hustler to enrich and magnify your life despite your background or current position.

Allow these codes to evoke your hustler's mentality so you can crack the hustle codes for yourself. You won't just learn how to play the game, but to own it. You will learn valuable principles to use as a guide in your daily existence. The Hustle Code promotes living life's potential to the utmost. Where life will serve you so you can really live for a change.

As an O.G. from the east side of Detroit, Michigan, a city with an infamous reputation for drug kingpins and notorious crime organizations, the author, Detroit King Tape, learned to hustle by growing up in the streets. His first lesson: Turns aren't given, they're taken. You can't wait for things to happen or for someone to give you something; you have to set it in motion yourself.

His experience from the school of hard knocks taught him unwritten rules that he codified to benefit all walks of life. He learned that it isn't just about surviving day-to-day life on the streets, but thriving as well! Don't you want to have your cake and eat it too? Sure you do. No question about it. And you don't even have to *like* cake. Take control of your world. The Hustle Code is your guide to excelling in your environment and creating a fulfilling reality.

The street principles the author compiled were intended to serve the next generation of hustlers he'd mentored. By earning the title O.G. and coming out on top in the underworld has led to his being acknowledged by youngsters and peers alike.

A serial entrepreneur, the author owns a variety of businesses, including his DWI record label and Ceenverde tequila brand. His colleagues, business partners, and associates were all impressed by his transformation. They see the author as a true success story. Their intrigue would always be followed by inquiry. *How did you turn your life around to benefit yourself and others in a positive way?* It was his hustle codes. The author saw that the codes could apply to anyone: business people, college students, homebodies, blu-collar workers, white-collar workers - anyone can use these hustle codes to accomplish their goals or have what they so desire.

Each chapter of The Hustle Code has an epigram or quote from the author, derived from previous works: music, books, and audio discourse. Following the quotes are anecdotes to introduce his ten hustle codes to the readers. The author also provides memoirs as examples for the readers to have a better understanding of the hustle codes, through his experience. These memoirs are short stories that do not follow a specific timeline or a chronological order. They are merely here to express in-depth examples of the author's experiences. Each chapter ends with an in-depth commentary and conclusions titled, "Bag It Up." Followed by the author's last words, "moving forward," is a section meant to encourage the reader to realize their potential as they journey through these hustle codes.

As a self-proclaimed straight shooter, he has included, Straight Talk and Notes to the readers who appreciate candidness and encouraging tips. It is notable to mention the author's ability to speak street and corporate jargon, respectfully, in practice to communicate ideas and form relationships. His dualistic manner of speech in this book is intended to appeal to readers on both sides of the AAVE fence: to those who are fluent in it, and those who are not. The core of each hustle code focuses directly on the mind. Although each code is different, all are interwoven fabric that protects and shields a hustler like Kevlar from slipping or getting taken by buzzard hustlers only out to capitalize off of a genuine hustler.

Recognizing the hustler in you will be a boost to your selfworth, showcasing the value you bring to the table. You are the currency! You are the product and natural resource! Train your mind with these hustle codes and watch your life *change*. Shape your reality as you imagine it could be; from a sheeple's mentality into that of a hustler.

DEFINITION OF A HUSTLER

*O*ne who obtains money by fraud or deceit:
SCAMMER, SWINDLER.

-Merriam Webster Dictionary

True Definition of a hustler

One who learns how to change the trajectory of their life. Using their mentality to outwit any opposing forces hindering their survival or success. One who knows how to take water and make wine. To Make something out of nothing. The know how to utilize every tool afforded to them; to persevere.

-Detroit King Tape

Chapter 1

ENVIRONMENT

"S ome look out their window and see a desert while others see a forest."

Let's cut to the chase. People are not the product of their external environment. Your surroundings do not solely dictate your mentality. The mind is forged by the environment first and foremost. Your mentality is composed of perception, conception, and imagination. Where thoughts, feelings, and behavior are rooted in an experience. A hustler is optimistic, thus having the ability to render his environment beneficial. The way you view your life will bring about the desired outcome. If you see it as unfair or bleak, your attitude and actions will create such circumstances. Your environment is malleable, and hustlers can create their own lanes no matter where they are in life.

MT. ELLIOT STREET

Somehow it feels good to stay clean,
When you grew up in shit!
    — IT'S HARD OUT HERE

Growing up on the Eastside of Detroit in the 80s was hard times for many: dilapidated homes, rundown businesses, and burnt apartment buildings left from the 1967 riots were my reality. My mother, older sister, younger brother, and I lived on Mt. Elliot Street in one of those rotten, wooden houses that shook off hazardous dust from the asbestos sidings onto the ground, which no doubt probably blew inside through the window cracks, filling the chipped lead-painted walls throughout the house. Not to mention dusting the piss-stained mattress that leaned against the side of my cousin's house around the corner, where we jumped and flipped on for fun.

Sometimes, we'd play at the graveyard up the street. It

was better than hanging out on the Heidelberg Project street. That's where this dude named Tyree Guyton splashed paint on a house and put hundreds of spooky dolls on it. It looked like something out of a Stephen King movie to me. *What the fuck was on his mind?* I thought.

TULLER STREET

Coming up I never wanted much,
long as we had enough;
But that didn't last long,
cause shit wasn't adding up!
                    — LORD KNOWS

My mother would drop me and my siblings off at my great grandmother's (Mommy Dear) house on the West Side for days on end. The houses in that neighborhood were mostly shabby, aluminum-siding homes. Mommy Dear's corner house was next to scrap yards, vehicle impoundment lots, and railroads off Lyndon Avenue. My mother's cousins also left their children with Mommy Dear. Other cousins, mostly older, lived there. I had a lot of fun with my cousins and friends on Tuller.

Us kids spent most of our time outside playing hide and seek or water games from the fire hydrant our older cousins turned on for us. We weren't allowed inside the house when the adults were there drinking liquor, smoking marijuana and cigarettes, and listening to "grown folk's music," what Mommy Dear called it. This would go on throughout the day and the greater part of the night. Somewhere in between we'd have dinner from food assistance meals from the Focus Hope charity program. Soon after we ate, we were sent back outside until the street lights came on. When we came back in, we had to go straight upstairs while the grownups carried on.

Going into the kitchen at night for a cup of water, I'd find myself in the middle of a horror film the instant I turned on the lights: an army of roaches would ransack the kitchen, then scatter in all directions across the worn tiles. It was a testament to a grim environment.

There was only one bathroom in the house, located downstairs. When the adults were down there partying, we had to use a piss bucket upstairs to relieve ourselves and empty it later when the house cleared. We also took turns sharing the bathtub before bedtime. It was up to a dozen children sleeping foot to head on a couple of twin beds and floor. On the weekends, the racket downstairs started in the late evening: loud music, swearing, and fights. Oddly, it sounded like good times to us children. Occasionally, the grownups would summon us downstairs to dance for them. My older cousins would tell neighborhood stories, and urban legends. We would crack jokes until we went to sleep.

EAST 7 MILE

I'm from the home of belle isle,
the road of 7 mile,
where niggas flip sacks to style,
we gotta stay sharp;
We don't give a fuck about how famous you are,
I'm from Detroit, dog, you betta know where you are!
— DETROIT SON

My mother moved us to a working-class neighborhood: brick bungalow houses, nice cars, and thriving businesses up and down East 7 Mile. We became the bougie family us kids joked about for not having roaches and rats. The corner stores were owned mostly by Arabs and taken over by winos begging for change. I didn't mind giving them a dollar to buy me and my friends liquor. It was a lively neighborhood; people were everywhere. It also was the height of the crack cocaine era.

Drug dealers gathered in front of neighborhood houses or

the Coney Island 24-hour restaurant, flaunting jewelry and new cars. Drug addicts roamed East 7 Mile all day and night carrying things they had stolen to sell for crack.

The hustle was all around me.

Stolen cars stripped in alleys, undercover prostitutes, people selling food stamps half-off for cash, and boosters selling hot designer clothing.

HIGH SCHOOL

I was taught that nothing comes to sleepers but dreams;
That's why I pulled all nighters in the spots with the fiends.
See me? I see shit from another perspective-
A hustlers perspective.
I see that brick as a necklace!

— MY LIFE MY HUSTLE

Osborn High School was an eye-opener. Fly girls with atti-
tudes, mostly sidity, and some of mixed-race. Dressed in the
latest fashion. Some of the dudes were as well; a few came to
school in their own cars. Students' cars didn't compare to the
older predator rides that parked in front of Osborn -- older guys
would wait for their tenderoni after school. They drove foreign
luxury vehicles and wore diamond-studded jewelry. Regular
school boys didn't stand a chance of getting a date with a fly girl
schoolmate, BKA , sack-chasers. The older guys also scooped
up young dudes in between class who were eager to sell drugs

for them in crack houses.

The winter would be my salvation. Snow shoveling those days was damn near a monopoly for a young enterprising teen such as myself. Other guys my age felt shoveling snow was whack, and beneath them. Acting like it's better to look cool on the porch with empty pockets. Other dudes were busy selling drugs. Making too much easy money to waste their time shoveling snow. My only competition was crackheads trying to shovel up on money to buy crack. I'd pass by them on the sidewalk with their heads hung low after the homeowners passed over the job to me. When I wasn't shoveling snow, I was working at a corner store, on 7 mile & Beland, counting 10cent soda bottles after school. I would have my friend's return bottles and hike up the count, so we could make an extra dollar or two. This was early on hustling for me.

At school, I'd bust a rap or two on the playground. Exciting the crowd was fun. Until your opponent's comeback, pulling out a wad of cash and calling you broke to an audience of fly girls. The crowd's cheers declaring the winner, tend to motivate a game-changer. Sometimes I wasn't even the one rapping. I was affected by the crowd's reaction, nonetheless.

My game changer happened while getting paid after shoveling snow. The homeowner dug inside her purse, sifting through hundred-dollar bills. I was excited by the sight of the Benjamins as she rummaged around, searching for ten dollars to square us off. Since that day, my hustle changed. I'd use my shovel as a ruse or prop, to B&E homes. I got my first taste of taking things into my own hands, literally. At the store, I'd line my jacket with stolen goods, after counting bottles. It was becoming more apparent to me that I benefited more from the by-any-means necessary method.

FUGITIVE

Mama I done killed a man,
ain't no repentance;
Since it's god's will,
he give killers forgiveness!?
                    — GANGSTA MUSIC

A person of interest for a homicide in Saginaw Michigan, I was on the run for three months. The paranoia of facing a life sentence didn't stop or slow my hustle. I still trafficked drugs and hung out at familiar stomping grounds. It was later ruled Justifiable Homicide. After the homicide detectives mocked the death of the habitual criminal of the robbery gone awry. Stating, that I'd did them a favor, and calling the deceased a "big gorilla." This gave me my first glimpse of just how cold & twisted our justice system is. Here I am, a teenager, sitting across from 2 homocide detectives, who are supposed to protect and serve, not crack jokes on a murder victim. Then pat the killer on the back. I left the interrogation room confused and feeling invincible. "*I just beat a body!*"

Not long after, I caught another case, a drug charge for Possession with the intent to distribute, in Mansfield, Ohio. I wound up serving 6 years in federal prison. As soon as the shackles were off my feet, I went straight back to my hustle. Three years later I was back on the run for three years for a State conspiracy charge in Traverse City, Michigan. That didn't stop anything. I hustled even harder.

RECORDING STUDIO

Got the block slapping,
nigga come thru clapping;
Real talk,
real rap,
man we ain't just rapping;
100 g's on the wristband,
200 keys and the bricks tan!
                    — BLOCK SLAPPIN'

I sold thousands of pounds of marijuana to support my rap career. I was living what I'd rapped about: cash, groupies, luxury cars, violence, and more violence. Sometimes the recording studio looked like public housing. Thugs and liquor bottles, smoke, guns and packed hallways. In the booth was my space, reciting lyrics. People loved what I said over underground beats. My music was intended to provide the listeners with an understanding of all that we go through trying to survive plus thrive in the hood.

Rapping opened doors for me. It allowed people to believe in something bigger than themselves. We didn't see rappers making it off of music from the hoods in Detroit. So, to see us pushing DWI records independently, but in a major way gave the people who saw me everyday hope. I would then take all that energy and hit the booth to rap about things that I needed to happen. I was speaking things into existence. A few of my partners thought I had a gift. Every time I went into the booth and rapped about having something (i.e. new car, crib, plug, etc.), it came to fruition. They didn't realize that I was purely manifesting. And the more people I got to chant this along with me, the more concentrated energy to make it happen.

FEDERAL PRISON

2 feet on the ground,
2 guns up high,
My mission is to aim for the sky.
If I get locked,
Shidd nigga don't cry,
Just let 'em know it's D.W.I.
                    — AIM FOR THE SKY

Federal prison warehouses the best hustlers who'd ever done it. Inside, it's all about prison life. Prison tools consist of, Weight pit, reading, religion, gangs, all sharpening criminal skills. Preying on the weak and embracing anger — the only real feelings left. I was fortunate to have met an inmate who was holistic and health conscious. He befriended me, and I began eating healthy. The benefits of becoming a vegan came swiftly. My body felt good inside and out. It cleared my vision. It allowed my natural physical and mental strength to unfurl. I began to measure myself to other prisoners and could easily determine how much stronger, quicker, and smarter I was than the average guy. I couldn't get enough of reading knowledge and self-awareness books. I became in tune with spirituality, albeit not religious. Reading poetry, philosophy and Black history books opened my mind. I could see beyond the prison's 20-foot walls. The ever-present dead gray tint that cast the prison's atmosphere appeared as lively colors through my mind's eye. Nearby doing morning calisthenics, not even the aggressive clanging of dumbbells in the weight pit could be heard from my serene standpoint. The hellish condition ran hot through everyone — prison guards included — rage, inflamed emotions, fiery words all insulated in concrete and steel. Changing the way I looked at things made my prison experience far less stressful. I applied what I learned at the Criminal University to the prison yard and immediately put it towards my hustle as soon as I got released.

STATE PRISON

I asked the lord why, you know we just killas with good hearts,
drug dealers with goals
We play the game how it goes,
Ima get money til the curtains is closed!
— HOMETOWN

Rhyming and hustling paid off for me in major ways. It took my hustle to various cities: Atlanta, Florida, Arizona, California, and the in-between. Eating healthy and living a plush life. High rises, condos, mansions, luxury cars, high-end restaurants, celebrity friends, industry chicks, everything VIP. Of course, I brought the hood with me. My homeboys with an East side, West side, Detroit state of mind. The places we had tore up and shut down—hotels, clubs, concerts, wherever we went. We lived up to the saying: "You can take a person out of the hood but not the hood out of a person." It wasn't long before I was back in prison for four more years.

Being vegan in prison proved harder the second time around, coming from eating nutrient-balanced meals to limited or no substitutions catered toward health. This was by far my biggest test. I was battling stress from every angle. I had children now. More responsibilities. I was no longer the teenager who had to learn from his mistakes. On top of

having a promising rap career in music, I had to get out. I fought for my freedom in the appellate courts until I won.

Four years later, I was finally granted a reversal in the Michigan State Supreme Court of Appeals. They overturned one of my conspiracy charges, and then ordered the trial judge to release me. This was not only a victory for myself, but also for other defendants as my case set a precedent. It was time to get back to the hustle.

HEALTH N HUSTLE

Calculated risks,
Making boss bets,
Logistics;
Importing shipments,
My attention on important business;
Health-n-hustle,
No mo struggling,
Investments doubling;
Til I get a billy ain't no cuddling!
　　　　　　　— GANGSTA/MILLIONAIRE

Back in the studio making music. Although my material hadn't changed, its message and inspiration transcended a hood mentality. I had billboards that expressed my record label's logo and motto. DWI records "We the ticket out of the hood." Evidence of my change also was seen in my company. My homeboys were affected by the positive energy. Now they had a professional attitude in the studio, and everyone wanted to take care of business rather than party. I turned Health-nHustle into a brand. It became a motivating factor in many people's lives close to me. The Health-N-Hustle principles became a guidepost. It shined on my personal relationships; with record execs and prominent people; so many positive interactions.

At one of my video shoots in Detroit, I drove Epic record execs through my old neighborhood. We stopped by the Heidelberg Project. They were amazed at the contrast of hope and desolation. I remember thinking, wow, Tyree Guyton is a man of vision. Who would've thought that a bunch of old dolls and tires would one day be recognized as art and monumental in the city of Detroit? Wow! Now I could see the flourishing future he imagined for my old neighborhood.

INTRODUCING LA

While Driving up the coast one afternoon as I'd done many times before, the palm trees, the ocean, the whole scene. It was like I was seeing it for the first time. I pulled my car over to a recluse beach and began feeding shorebirds sunflower seeds as I stood in shallow water, still in my shoes, enjoying life as never before... Everything was new from then on.

STRAIGHT TALK

As a prisoner, I found a way to change my mental environment.

This allowed me to see the bigger picture and not get caught up in the day-to-day BS of prison politics and the frustrations of being in physical slavery.

I have a friend who is currently doing a life sentence. He would run a prison store stocking up on food and extra commissary to sell or loan out to prisoners for extra. This is how he made money to survive. Every week when other inmates got their commissary, he would collect from them. He would open his cell door and blast my music (from a cassette tape we smuggled in through the prison church) while the people who borrowed from him came to pay their debts. Those who didn't pay saw a different person. The doors would close, and he would fuck them up. It was known that if you borrow from his store, you better pay up. I saw him in action. I pulled him to the side one day and told him "If you plan on going home one day, don't allow a ramen noodle to stop you from gaining your freedom. Long story short, he took my advice and started running his store differently. He's been incarcerated now for 22 years. With the help of the Innocence Project, he is scheduled to get his life sentence overturned in the next few years. To add he has earned numerous certifications, college credits and has become a notable speaker at different colleges. All from inside the prison walls, due to him changing his perception.

You can allow your environment to turn you into an animal, or you can use your mind to take the mental shackles away, allowing you to place precedence on the bigger goal at hand. A hustler has to first assess every component of his environment;

to evaluate all that can be deemed useful or useless. Combining what is useful with his/her skill set to either create a product or service and then zero in on the demand.

BAG IT UP

The belief that we are products of our environment is a gross disservice to ourselves and our interaction with others. It takes away self-control and surrenders it to prejudice and misconception.

The majority designates which environment shall be heaven or hell:

Public housing over here; condominiums over there; red district in this area; upscale neighborhood in that area.

Buying into such devised conditions you may not have considered that the inner city doesn't necessitate run-down homes and poverty no more than suburbia has to be safe and affluent. Our conduct always reflects our environment. Bullets and crime tend to accompany blight and dilapidation in the inner cities, whereas peace, calm, and intact homes fill the outskirts. It explains why people are quick to break laws on East 7 Mile in the city but abide by every public ordinance when they cross 8 Mile in the burbs. This is learned behavior.

This code does not suggest you live under delusions. Yes, duck when gunfire is heard; move your family to a safe location when able. Where one person or group imposes their mental environment on us, know that you can push back. Take into consideration that if the majority of people are living a certain way, that can affect you and your loved ones. Do not be naive to think that you will not become a statistic. If you live on a battlefield. There will be casualties. All it takes is one individual to spark inspiration in others to see your vision. Remember: majority rules.

MOVING FORWARD

Your environment should fuel you to boss up /level up. If you are looking out the window at blight, chaos, or danger, this should motivate you to overcome the fear of your environment. Dig deep and seek the answers to change those abandoned houses into paradise and palm trees. You have a choice to either change your environment or complain and wallow in filth. Some people are stuck in a complaining mentality which never changes anything. What it does is aggravate the situation and circumstances. Once you accept the fact that your environment is a problem, then and only then can you initiate the necessary tools for a change.

Simply put, you take two individuals and place them in the same environment, and they can have totally different outcomes.

Your mindset creates your environment.

***NOTE: IT'S IMPERATIVE TO UNDERSTAND THAT ADAPTING TO YOUR ENVIRONMENT IS AN

ACT OF SIMPLY TRYING TO MAKE LIFE EASIER OR INCREASING YOUR CHANCES OF SURVIVAL!

(EVOLUTIONARY ADAPTATION)

OUR GOAL IN THIS CHAPTER IS TO AWAKEN THE MINDSET OF THE READER TO NOT JUST THINK OF MERELY SURVIVING IN SOMEONE ELSE'S ENVIRONMENT BUT TO THINK INDEPENDENTLY ENOUGH TO CREATE THEIR OWN ENVIRONMENT THAT SERVES THEM AND THEIR PURPOSE IN LIFE.

Chapter 2

FEAR

"**T**he only thing to fear is dying silent — your voice should make the earth shake in life and death."

Fear is conceived through the mind-body complex, a product of our thoughts and feelings. Though fear itself is an illusion, it still spreads like a virus. It is your mental environment that makes fear seem real. Depending on how you perceive it. People are trained to fear. Contrary to popular belief, it has been promoted that fear is healthy to scare people to behave in a manner society deems right or correct. In reality, fear is not healthy due to its underlying stress, striking at your wellness. I have found, however, that it is necessary for selfpreservation. A hustler does not fear consequences but only considers them before taking action. Own your fear and life will yield to your advantage.

HOME TRAINED

G-shit all in my DNA,
It's all in my veins;
Pops got locked,
OG game me the game,
Hit the block with the bag,
An OG I became;
50 thousand in a month to keep me entertained!
　　　　　—LIFE IN THE D

When I was four or five years old, my father used to dress me in suits, ties, and dobbs hats. I was this mini version of how he saw himself: as a gangster and pimp. The memories I have of him are few and far between. He was in prison most of my life. The vivid memory I have of my father on this side of the fence was him beating the shit out of me for drinking his liquor. He had left a glass on the living room table., and I made the gross mistake of thinking he'd left that for me. He came back from the kitchen, saw the glass half empty, and went into a rage. He whipped me like I stole something.

My mother often expressed that she did not want me to be like my father. She reiterated this through the whoopings I received from her. Maybe she saw me as my father's spitting image. My said-to-be good features- which were referenced in the black family as fair skin- straight, curly, or manageable hair plus smaller lips and nose was a conversation topic for my mother and her friends. Her friends would praise her for raising a little lady's man as she kept me up, putting a jerry curl in my hair til 3am on a school night. It was picture day and she wanted me to look good.

My mother's whoopings were epic. She had bought me some new clothes one day for a holiday. We were all going to Belle Isle. Before we left, my cousin and I went to play at the graveyard, coming home filthy. We would ride our bikes to the Mount Elliott Cemetery to see the headstones and try to catch tadpoles. When we returned, all I remember was my mother yelling at me, then I saw blue and black stars. Granted I was bad as hell, yet my mother's whippings were confusing. Was she tryna beat my father out of me? Or just taking her problems out on me?

One day my mother made it clear to me and my brother that she was not "raising no snitches or no punks" and that she would kill us before she'll ever allow us to become one. She didn't have to beat it in me; her threats were enough for me to have fear just the same. My mother was also adamant about me not being like the guys she'd dated. Street hustlers were her type. I admired them for having a pocket full of money, nice cars, being well-dressed, and having good-looking women like my mother on their arms. I picked up on these same traits and characteristics as this became me as I got older. Once grown, I realized that my mother's tough love and discipline was preparing me to face certain fears and adversities as a young black man in America.

OFF THE PORCH

Recurring nightmares of the police,
The life I chose shidd it could never be peace;
When it's all said and done it's either them or me,
Pac era Hennessy and penitentiaries; ·
Cheat if I have to, to win,
Fuck all yo penalties,
I'm a god, can't no other man deliver me!
— NO, NO, NO

I didn't do those B&E's for the sake of adrenaline rushes, nor did I have something to prove to anyone. I kept my mouth shut about it. What I liked was being able to buy nice things. Sometimes, I had to wait for the people who lived in the houses I'd case to leave. I often became frustrated with how people were always running late. *"Hurry up so I can rob you I thought!"* At times I was in freezing weather or thorn bushes. I outright looked suspicious walking up and down the block trying to look inconspicuous. Factors that should have made me forget about it and get another hustle. Yet I knew that patience was a virtue and going on a dry run wasn't an option. How about prying open back or side windows, climbing inside, not really knowing who's there? Maybe they'd have a gun?

Looking for the safe and duffle bags. All at a neck-breaking pace while pocketing jewelry and tucking guns. What a relief to have made it home with the goods. Watching my brother's happy expression when I gave him stuff. My mother's lips curled tight, but she still accepted my offerings. It made my day. Making her smile, even grudgingly, was worth the risk.

TOXIC

Hardships hardened my heart and I left 'em bleeding,
didn't mean to leave when you needed me;
I was tryna make this hard shit easy,
I know I can make this hard shit easy!

— EASY

Damaged relationships

Scenario 1

Sweetwater Tavern was always a good place to go for lunch and socializing. Once, I met an attractive young woman there. We had a pleasant conversation. She shared her recent ordeal with me: a drug deal gone bad, robbery, captivity, and being tossed out to the roadside by her assailants. I bought her lunch and a couple of shots; she needed it after what she had been through.

We ended up spending the day together. She had such a strong will and great spirit. I got to know her, and we eventually got involved. She was trusting and loyal to a fault. Her daddy issues somehow were appealing to me. Our relationship was short-lived, despite hooking up from time to time. In truth, I saw my mother in her, a woman in need of a knight in shining armor. A damsel in distress.

Scenario 2

At a strip club, I locked eyes with an exotic-looking waitress. I was there with business associates, and I didn't have time to mingle. A week or so had passed before I went back there again to conduct business. That waitress and I remembered one another. We instantly connected and had so much in common. Like prison time.

She had served time for trafficking marijuana. Right up my alley. The people she'd been working for had left her on the meat hook. She was abandoned at a young age by her birth parents and later adopted. I wasn't only attracted to her looks, but her mind as well. She was smart and a fast learner. Clingy too, but I didn't mind. Her tantrums irritated me, and she'd become mad for not coming to bed after a hard day of hustling. Throwing fits when I'd go to the studio without her, and other nuisances. I felt she didn't appreciate when we'd come into each other's lives when she needed a companion. Ultimately, it ended because of the stress and drama.

Scenario 3

I met an older woman. She was loyal and a survivor. Her dedication to following the plan to the letter and aerobics regiment was what appealed to me the most about her. As much as we vibed and could converse on many topics, there wasn't much I could do for her. Despite her life being in order, she often complained that I didn't spend money or support her as she was accustomed to. Really, she wasn't open to letting a man take the lead, taking pride in being an independent woman. During Our last argument, she said, "Don't punish me for having my shit together unlike your past relationships." In a manner of speaking, I was out the door, I had somewhere else to be. In all honesty, she was right. I only felt the need to help women who I knew needed my help. The women who I saw my mother in.

PAYOFF

Gotta get back to you later,
Right now I'm getting to the paper;
I'm paranoid I hate neighbors,
I did the plug 100 favors!

— WANT

Coming back from my out-of-town hustle was always exciting. Cashed up, making a ritual of going to the mall and shopping for the latest fashion. Calling my jeweler up and buying a new car through my broker, just to go back to the old neighborhood and be seen. Eyeballs would lock on me from hat to shoes. I would drive to a familiar carwash or two. Hit some blocks, pull up on a few females — let it be known that I was back in town. People would act happy when they saw me. Saying shit like, " You made it, man." The hood mentality, living for self-image and accolades.

SOLO

I done seen and put in so much work,
That I'm immune to the shit that hurt;
This paper chase is a race. I gotta get it first!
— WIN

I started off doing robberies with my crew. The bigger the jobs, the more confident I became. I saw jealousy building from certain individuals I committed robberies with. This brought about disagreements on how we would commit the robberies. It had gotten to the point that I was doing major robberies by myself. In fact, hitting licks alone was a relief. I no longer had the paranoia of being robbed while robbing a place. We all stuffed our pockets and hid valuables on robberies. Lying through our teeth to one another. Damn near killing each other to prove the other was lying. It was a dirty game that I was tired of playing. Committing home invasions and not having anyone to watch my back, took balls. The adrenaline pushed me through, coming back with all that loot, rubbing it in their faces. Feeling I had the biggest nuts. My new attitude spilled over into life.

A FEW REAL ONES

Driving down this road,
That I've been on for years;
Imagine how much stress I've been thru,
I've been on for years;
Been living with this fear,
Of better get money nigga;
Or you gon die like yo pops with no money!
— GETTING MONEY

Moving pounds of marijuana from state to state while on the run from US Marshalls and Feds, I headed to Atlanta with a tire stuffed with B.C. Marijuana. I ended up getting pulled over in Tennessee by the D.E.U. (Drug Enforcement Unit). They searched the truck for 2 hours but came up empty-handed. The tire was sealed tight. I told myself, "I gotta stop thinking I can do it all by myself." I was so pissed off when the person who was supposed to drive canceled on me. I decided, fuck it, I'll do it myself. This error in thinking continued to cost me for years down the line.

LOSE TO GAIN

I've lost and had to take,
Learned from others mistakes;
Gotta know when to break niggas or give them a break!
　　　　　— GANGSTA MUSIC

I made a hard decision to sell my BMW for 200 lbs of Arizona popcorn weed. I shipped my vehicle to Arizona and waited for the Mexicans. Before I could get the package, I got locked up. After being on the run for 3 years I got picked up on a random traffic stop. Once they ran my fingerprints. It was off to jail where I had to face the music. The Mexican deal fell through due to me not being able to oversee the operation from the county jail. The money I was able to collect didn't even amount to the car's worth. I wound up paying lawyers off with the money.

When the feds finally caught me, pressure weighed heavily on my shoulders. People depended on me. My family, my team, girlfriends, and the customers to whom I supplied marijuana. Somehow in that prison cell, my stress had been relieved. Although I could breathe easier, it was hard realizing that I couldn't do shit about what was going on in the free world. The ton of bricks from feeling obligated and responsible for so many others would only fall off after I exhausted every possible way to help, even though I was the one who needed help.

I started hustling inside the prison, smuggling. I also ran street operations from the restrictions of county jail, through my brother. Together, we flipped the packages into nice profits. My bounce-back quality strengthened my drive to never stop the hustle.

RECKLESS

I'm a rare find,
Gangsta with a great mind;
Plug outta sight,
With the killas on stand by;
He's a lie if he say he got Tape;
Told the feds to they face they'll never catch me on tape!
                    — NARCO DREAMS

Elkton Ohio federal prison, me and my cellmate devised a plan to smuggle marijuana into the prison through the visiting room. The package came through like clockwork. Until one time the visitor left the ounces in the trash instead. I created a tool to unscrew the handicap rail in the women's visiting room bathroom. Where they could unscrew the rail, place the ounces inside and screw them back in. For some reason they couldn't get the screw loose, so they had to leave the marijuana in the trash can. Big mistake... The C.O. Had us throw the trash in the bin, which was just beyond the prison fence. My persistence wouldn't allow me to let my masterplan be foiled. We hyped ourselves up to hop the fence to retrieve the package. That very instant it dawned on me. What the fuck am I doing? I was serving a meatball, (a short prison sentence) — less than a couple of years left. I could get charged with escape — an automatic five years tacked on the time I already was serving. Plus, we could have gotten killed! I reassessed the situation and quickly jumped my ass back over the fence.

Feeling defeated, I went back to my cell.

This realization/wake-up call helped me get through my time to be eligible to get Back out and back at it. I epitomized that saying, "work hard, play harder." Up early making money and spending it at night in the clubs. It had gotten to the point where I'd have people bring money they'd owed me there. Caught up in the moment, I made it a habit of spending thousands, drinks, strippers, tips, and partying. The next day, I had to double down to recoup the money I had thrown in the air.

Living as if the hustle would never slow down.

REFINING

My people going broke
From overspending,
Over shopping;
On dumb shit,
That's why I'm starting business to profit!

— WIN

Difference in Mindsets

Scenario 1

At the club with associates having a good time as they tossed thousands of dollars in the air. The next morning, an opportunity presented itself to make a few hundred thousand.

I contacted my associates from the night before at the club.

None of them had enough money to buy into the great opportunity. But they were throwing away thousands at the club. Thousands, which could've been invested to make 4-500% returns.

Scenario 2

My friend/partner in the luxury rental car business in Los Angeles. Whenever friends came to town, I'd let them drive luxury vehicles through LA. Some had video shoots or filming projects they were working on. I extended the same courtesy that had been given to me.

One day, my partner brought it to my attention that I shouldn't risk our business and personal relationship by allowing someone else to fuck up a half of million-dollar vehicle. Then it hit me. He's right. I'd let a friend borrow my Cadillac SUV once. He'd have crumbs and food bags all on the seats and floor; it reeked of liquor and marijuana. He drove the rubber off the tires, fucked up my rims, resulting in my truck getting towed and impounded. Moral of the story: Never let anyone ruin your good connections due to their irresponsibility. Also, stop giving things to people who do not take care of their own property.

BILLIONAIRES MENTALITY

All I got is my balls and my word and my intuition;
I see billions through these lenses,
Big business
And boss decisions!
         — DROP THAT LOCATION

I was having lunch with a millionaire friend. We were comparing schedules, and I told him I had to hit the mall, see my jeweler, and get ready for the studio. He pointed out that I seemed committed to spending more money than making money. He said he would start each morning with breakfast, stretching exercises, and thinking of ways that he can make more money vs money spent. He broke down his strategy when it came to his monthly bills. If he had 50K in bills per month, he'd be determined to make $1,700 per day to cover his bills. Anything else was extra.

STRAIGHT TALK

Some are terrified of people, places, things, or situations while others acknowledge and accept the danger of that fear without recourse. Take a person who is deathly afraid of sharks, while another person will swim in a vast ocean of great whites.

You'll find similar scenarios in just about everything from fear of guns to fear of heights.

Consider the Buddhist monk who set himself on fire. He had to reach a pinnacle level of nonexistent fear. His mind had to override the pain of being burned alive. While an extreme example, I felt the need to use this to exemplify the true power of the mind. How many times have you stubbed your toe? Hit your elbow, or had a fast-jolting pain in an area of your body? What was your reaction? Was there an outburst? Did you feel that pain?

I remember accidentally shooting myself. After an argument with my brother over money and disrespect. I pulled my gun, attempting to shoot him. You may be asking yourself; how could you do that? Just know that disrespect isn't tolerated in the hood. Regardless of blood relations or not. This is a direct test of a man's ego and manhood. Which must be addressed and checked by any means necessary. Even if it means losing your life. I couldn't sleep at night knowing I allowed someone to disrespect me. Whether verbally or physically. Disrespect in any form is unacceptable. I remember telling my mother that I was going to shoot my brother for his disrespect. I told her I wasn't going to kill him. Though he had to learn a lesson. My mentality was geared toward protecting a false image of self-respect and what we dreamed of as manhood. It all happened, when I finally saw my brother driving up Whitehill Street, after leaving the car wash. Words were exchanged, guns were drawn, followed by a high-speed chase through the streets of the east side. I fired shot after shot, with my left hand as I trailed his car while trying to catch him. To no avail. Once I snapped out of my rage, I came to my senses and slowed the car down. Still driving, while attempting to decock the p89 ruger; the hammer slipped, and the gun went off. All I remember was the smoke rising from the top of my gym shoe. The burning from the misguided slug was extremely painful. It felt as if someone poured hot lava on my foot. I had to use a tactic we call "psyching yourself out" in order to calm down the intense throbbing. To my surprise, it was working. Until I had to move or put pressure on my foot on my way to the hospital. Its ironic that my brother, (whom I was shooting at), had to come pick me up and take me to the hospital. This situation had gone too far. At this moment, I realized how stupid this entire incident was. My fear of being disrespected, almost made me kill my brother. Aside from the tons of regret, this taught me an important skill: how to use my mind to push past the pain. I would later apply this to various situations throughout my life. From overcoming obstacles in business to heartbreak or physical pain. Most survivors build a high level of tolerance for pain, due to overcoming the most arduous situations. As a hustler, it's key to use your mind to acknowledge the fear of whatever task lies ahead. Then accept that fear, even if the danger is still present. Remember it's all about how you train your mind to respond to the fear that arises.

BAG IT UP

Our senses are natural receivers, highly adapted to our mental and physical environment. What we see, taste, touch, hear, and smell are processed for mental interpretation. Where everything received initially is seen as a threat to selfpreservation until we reason it's not harmful. Pain hurts both physically and emotionally. We remember what caused us to suffer. We tend to avoid painful memories, on high alert for anything perceived as a potential threat.

It's between the gaps of painful memories and the space between future threats where we invent fear. Past experiences can keep us on guard for the future, allowing for missed opportunities. The problem is that our past hazards rely on selective memories and our future perils rely on imagination. Both past and future are products of the mind just as imagination and memories. How little we remember and so much we fabricate. Fear of losing property, valuables, reputation, our youth, etc., is debilitating. It interferes with progress, advancement, advantages, esteem, and performance.

It can be stated a failure to recall does not mean it didn't happen. The actual pain and trauma, yes. But what happened to the fear? It disappears as an illusion. Like the fear of being fired after actually getting fired. Or the fear of losing money once your stock investment has plummeted. The fear of your Ferrari getting stolen when it already had been stolen. Fear does not exist before just like it does not afterwards. Your mind makes it real. A threat can be real, no doubt. But fear will drive you insane.

MOVING FORWARD

Your fear is the deciding factor to change or remain isolated inside a mental prison that you have created for yourself. Right now, you can turn that fear into the hustler's aggression that's needed to be your driving force to get shit done in life. Create distance between yourself and the fear of being in harm's way. Whether it is poverty, debt, drama, failure, heartbreak, or any emotion that is triggered by you not being the best version of yourself. Normalize turning on the light in the spooky dark basement that you are so afraid to go down. It's all in your mind. As soon as the light comes on, you realize nothing is there. Knowing who you are and what you are capable of helps you face your fears head-on. There is another side to fear associated with hustling. Ex: How many of us are generous, kind-hearted, etc. These types of people tend to be taken advantage of. Therefore, giving them the mentality of "I'm no longer helping anyone." That's self-sabotaging to a hustler's grind. I call this being game-conscious. Where a hustler will pass up on great opportunities from being fearful of losing out or getting ripped off like before.

NOTE: DO NOT CARRY YOUR LAST DEAL OVER TO YOUR CURRENT OR FUTURE DEALS. DOING THIS WILL ALREADY SET THE ENERGY OF THE DEAL. BE PRECAUTIOUS, THO NOT GAME-CON-SCIOUS. NEVER LEAD WITH FEAR. IF YOU FEAR A DEAL. YOU SHOULDN'T BE DOING IT. IT'S A FACT, THAT FEAR DECREASES ANY CHANCES OF EXECUT-ING A TASK WITH CONFIDENCE.

Chapter 3

AGGRESSION

"The timid get intimidated. Intimidation is for the timid."

A hustler's aggression is the raw energy behind your thoughts, words, and actions, prompting you to perform assertively. It is a hustler's power punch to knock out obstacles blocking accomplishments. Without a hustler's aggression, you won't be fully capable of protecting what matters to you the most: honor, respect, tradition, livelihood, family — anything that you value. Be aware of other attributes of aggression: "intelligent aggression" and flawed aggression. Flawed aggression is counter-productive, selfish and for the most part, self-defeating. Intelligent aggression is goal-oriented, more concerned about the group or team succeeding than just him/herself. A hustler who practices intelligent aggression does it with confidence.

RAW & UNCUT

Call it progression,
Fuck a recession;
Getting money dog-
Is how I channel my aggression!
— TELL ME SHIT

My middle-class neighborhood had turned into a slum. I was too entrenched in contributing to its demise to even have seen what was occurring right before my eyes. I was busy setting up shop in willing tenants' homes or vacant houses. When one drug house mysteriously caught on fire, we'd go to the next one on that block. Eventually, an entire street was a pile of rubbish and ashes. It reflected my mentality.

Mean mugs and cold stares on every street; bullet holes in street signs; dead people's shoes hanging from electric lines; gunshots heard throughout the day and night, followed by EMS and police sirens. The mere mention of outsiders coming to our neighborhood and setting up shop on the real estate we claimed – east 7 Mile. It was an act of war where we would evoke the 2nd Amendment to shut that shit down. No one ever had to convince one another; the attitude came with the turf.

GOOD, BAD & UGLY

Tryna bring a million home
Plus minus the conflict;
The nonsense made me a convict,
My conscience made money my topic;
A presidential nigga with politics,
I see way past the block shit!

— THE INTERVIEW

As soon as the prison gates opened, my children's mother was in the parking lot waiting for me in a used Ford Explorer. It was an eyesore. I always had her driving up-to-date cars.

Immediately, the pressure was on me.

I didn't report straight to the parole office. I had her take me to my old neighborhood to touch base with associates. I could see it was tight for everyone. A total contrast to what I'd believed in prison. My guys were all trying to come up with a plan to make a lot of money. They looked to me to put things back together despite my just returning to society after serving four years. More pressure.

Later that night, my guys took me to a familiar club. As soon as I stepped inside, I received hugs and handshakes from people I knew one way or the other. The DJ gave me a shot out, mixed, and played some of my music. Bottles were sent to my booth by former street associates and hustlers; dancers rushed to our booth giving me welcome back lap dances. It was hard for me to enjoy the moment. Deep down I knew I really wasn't living up to the praise. The night ended in the emergency room with staples in the back of my head, from mixing lean, alcohol and smoking, resulting in me passing out, and hitting my head from falling.

GOOD

We understood what life means,
That's why we share the good that life brings,
Let nothing;
Come between this thing of ours,
If so-
Bring flowers,
We'll shower them cowards!

— THE INTERVIEW

My brother and I were driving back from picking up a serious bag. It was a typical 9 to 5 Detroit afternoon. We watched for any opposition that would prevent us from reaching our goal.

Really our concerns were more about driving the speed limit and making roughly 80k off of this flip than being nervous about getting stopped by the police.

BAD

We run it up
Just to fuck it up,
fuck rap nigga,
We trap niggas;
Thumbs hurting from the paper cuts,
Keep the pole on me just to clap niggas;
Them bricks come and they stamped nigga,
I'm stamped all around the map nigga;
Work the heavy bag I'm the champ nigga,
Bigger than rap facts nigga!

— WHAT YOU GONE DO

I received a call from my son's mother while driving. No hello, how are you, be safe; she started off with bullshit! The argument had gotten so intense, that I took the next exit to make a U-Turn.

UGLY

I know somehow someway
Niggas gotta make it out the game one day;
My nigga just survived 2 shots with a K,
We prayed I guess that prayer brought my Nigga home safe;
But fuck that-
I would've rather he died;
Cause after that the judge hit my nigga with life;
And all he wanted to be was a soldier a soldier,
All he wanted to be was a soldier like me!

— LOVE OF THE GAME

The phone call had left me distracted, ignoring any traffic laws. Whatever my brother was saying to me flew straight out the car window. All I could see was red with a deafening sound of rage. The thought that if we got caught is a life sentence was tossed around in the backseat with the bag of drugs.

The closer I got to my child's mother's house, the more

callous I became and less concerned about the business or our freedom. I didn't know what I was going to do when I got there. She really knew how to push my buttons. I was ready to risk it all to prove a point that was pointless.

STRAIGHT TALK

We associate aggression with primarily anger. Rarely do we classify an ambitious person closing a deal as aggressive. Now let's change your train of thought. A hustler's aggression is expressed in his/her passion for their hustle/trade. It can be their excitement to create, execute, or close that deal. It is their creative energy turned up to the max. As for myself, I get turnt up every time I'm working on a project. I normally only sign on to projects that inspire or motivate me. Especially when in the studio recording a song. Once I vibe with the beat, my hustler's aggression kicks in. To help me dig deep in my mind for the best bars. During a session with a multiple platinum artist, who was a good friend of mine, we were searching for the right beat to record on. He schooled me. He said, "If the beat doesn't catch your attention within the first three seconds, move on to the next one." I adopted this practice and it stuck with me ever since. I began to apply this same approach to business ventures/ ideas. You should feel inspired to be a part of a project. You may be rehabbing a house. Or working on a filming project. A car, investment, etc. You should be interested from the moment you learn about it. If a project takes a lot of convincing, nine times out of ten, you are going to need continuous convincing throughout the process. This will in turn complicate the project, and most likely create a dislike or regret of ever committing to the project.

Acknowledge your hustler's aggression. Pay attention to yourself and others when you either see it or feel it. It is blood in the water to a shark.

BAG IT UP

The hustler's aggression as expressed through words and actions is done with a sense of purpose. It's an intelligent approach to execute the hustle; by communicating the overall mission with associates, delegating tasks, and going against all odds to succeed.

The hustler's aggression rises above mere fear or frustration; such simple aggression is too emotional for a hustler to operate efficiently and with a clear head. However, a hustler is able to channel raw, simple aggression into smart ways to accomplish goals.

There are two other attributes of aggression that a hustler has as an option to apply to the hustle. Good and bad aggression; whichever best fits your agenda and proves most effective.

Bad aggression is counterproductive in nature, not because it's bound to fail, but its implications from the start. It's probable that it'll be a one-time score. This category of aggression is best prescribed for a solo hustler or for a hustler with an "all or nothing" attitude, sacrificing the whole of the little to gain a lot.

Good aggression is most useful for a hustler with a vision and a team spirit. This type of hustler's aggression gives a way to all to benefit.

MOVING FORWARD

Hustler's Aggression is the door opener and the closer. Life is a ride—- just get gas. This is the motto of Hustler's Aggression. This is the deciding factor for the undecided. The "fuck it, let's go! It's my time. If not now, then when?" This code pairs well with self-belief/confidence. This gives you the ability to move when there is hesitation in your movement. This creates motion. No more sitting on your hands. Stand on your feet and make it happen!

****NOTE: EMOTIONS ARE ENERGY. THE GOAL IS TO ACKNOWLEDGE THESE EMOTIONS AND THEN USE THEM TO YOUR ADVANTAGE. LEARN HOW TO CHANNEL YOUR AGGRESSION AND DIRECT IT TOWARD A GOAL. THIS CONCENTRATED EFFORT WILL PROVE EFFECTIVE AND PRODUCTIVE. WHEN YOU FIND YOURSELF ANGERED OR IRRITATED, FIND A WAY TO TAKE THAT ENERGY AND USE IT TO KILL THE GAME INSTEAD OF KILLING SOME-ONE.

Chapter 4

OPPORTUNITY

"Opportunity never knocks softly —it damn near kicks your door down."

Everyone is guilty of taking an opportunity, but a hustler isn't afraid to admit it. Exploiting chance for one's advancement; taking advantage of the spur-of-the-moment. However, a hustler knows it's not in your best interest to be an opportunist. There are two kinds of hustlers: lions and buzzards.

Lion hustlers use tact and morals when endeavoring to gain. Otherwise, it's a pyrrhic victory at the cost of losing the trust and voucher from associates — the very building stones a lion hustler values to succeed. Lions recognize that an opportunity to profit at the expense of others often results in a stoppage to one's rise and credibility.

The actions of a buzzard hustler, preying on someone's downfall for the chance to eat, is a conscious decision to burn bridges. Such desperate acts often prove to be career-ending moves. Should there ever come a time when opportunity calls, always answer with a lion hustler's sureness and take the opportunity a prey has offered. Make a merciful kill, then break bread with pride.

BUZZARD

We deadly victims of hate crime; Haters will kill you cause they can't shine!
— WELCOME TO DETROIT CITY

At a prestigious Hollywood event with celebrity friends and business acquaintances, I was spotted by an associate and his companions. He had an extensive cannabis operation in the works. He wanted me to liaison his dispensary operation, and for my celebrity friend to be the face of his cannabis brand. As a professional courtesy, I passed the message along. My celebrity friend had no kind words to say about his approach and intentions, quoting, "He don't give a fuck about us – that guys an opportunist!"

LIONS

We down to get that money
But that money never made us;
Hard work pays off,
Yeah the blocks paid us;
Everything paid off,
Either that or paid up;
Late nights on the road kept a nigga staying up,
Kept a nigga papered up,
Kept a nigga weighing up;
We knew that we was good if the fiend gave it 8 or up!
— BALLING

Some of my Hollywood associates shared with me their involvement in a documentary of notable writer Donald

Goines. I expressed my familiarity with his work; being from the same city and reading his novels while being incarcerated.

I offered my input and resources that could assist them with the project. They genuinely offered me a partnership in the film. I accepted.

MERCIFUL

I'm into real sport,
We tryna fill vaults;
To fill the void of the shit I lost,
But still I fought;
Everything from murder to conspiracy-
The fear of god couldn't even put the fear in me!
                        — LIFE IN THE D

I was making a video for my song "Yeah." The videographer
I'd worked with previously, had a full schedule. I shopped
around and linked with a credible videographer through a go-
between. The middleman thought it would be an opportunity
for him to up the price on me. After a conversation with the
videographer, we came to a price agreement. I still paid the
middleman what I thought was fair for him connecting me
to the videographer, and not the price he tried to put on top
of the videographer's quote. Although it was not the amount

he expected, I made sure he made something for his efforts. I could have told him to get lost, but instead, I was hoping he learned a valuable lesson in doing good business.

STRAIGHT TALK

A hustler never shuns an opportunity. He considers every opportunity even if every opportunity doesn't strike my interest. Instead, I use clarity to evaluate the opportunity to see who I can pass it along to. It's like an assist in the NBA: the opportunity is the ball. The basketball court is the environment. When an opportunity presents itself, see who is open that you can pass the ball to for an easy score. Learn how to become the Magic Johnson of opportunities. Remember that an assist only counts if the hustler you pass the ball to scores. Be very selective in who you pass it to. This can cause you to either win or lose the game. Once you accept the opportunity, you have committed to being part of the game. Your name will be associated with the outcome. So, choose wisely.

Note: All of the hustle codes coincide and collectively work together in a joint effort of mastery.

BAG IT UP

A hustler is swift to take advantage of an opportunity that could advance or promote the mission. Knowing it's not every day that the right set of circumstances would present themselves in your favor. It is synergetic when all the pieces come together and everything lines up. For this reason, you should never pass up a full opportunity — regret is certain to arise with calamity to the mission. A hustler serves the hustle and vice versa; it's a give-and-take relationship. Time, capital, sweat equity, and security. In return, your hustle provides you with position and power. This makes hustle a divine profession as it bestows blessings and offerings that are god-like. If you neglect or abuse your livelihood, it will reciprocate, causing you loss and damage. Missed opportunities are gross negligence. Accept any and all opportunities that push your agenda forward. Never wait or stop the hustle until everything aligns. However, realize some opportunities should be passed up as they can wreak of counter productivity. Unfortunately, opportunity does not promise a favorable or unfavorable outcome but is decided by your execution, and or how well you perform.

Consider these two forms of opportunism before taking action: buzzard hustle and lion hustle. The buzzard hustler lurks in the cuts and crevices, waiting for an opportunity to fall at its feet to pick its bones. It's futile to wait for an opportunity to manifest. To do so is to neglect your hustle. Even being too picky about an opportunity can prove unprofitable. Beware of making a habit of missed opportunities, as it makes a hustler timid or passive. In any case, the buzzard hustle, a lazy and wasteful approach from a go-getter perspective, is selfish in nature and doesn't prompt others to elevate or share in bread-breaking.

A lion hustler, however, accepts the opportunity as an offering. A sacred act worthy of respect and sometimes, sacrifice. Like a lion in the Sahara, it surveys and marks its territory; bonds with hunter lionesses and grooms his cubs. In other words, they stay focused on the goal, and when opportunity comes, lions are ready, swift, and frugal, never wasting time, energy, or what's on their plates. The lion's collective effort and shared meals should also be your mentality in acquiring wealth and longevity.

MOVING FORWARD

Opportunism is based on perfect timing created by proper decision-making. You rarely stumble upon an opportunity. Even when you think a perfect opportunity just came out of nowhere, check yourself, because it did not. Give yourself some credit—you had to be in the right place at the right time. That quick decision to make that sharp right turn puts you where you needed to be ten minutes earlier. Had you not been there, someone else may have gotten that opportunity. If you have been setting things in motion over time, two things will happen: either it worked or it didn't. The light will be green or red, depending on how in tune you are with the universe and the inner workings of your will/mind. This requires a hustler's intuition. Tap into those feelings to guide you to those opportunities. Lay the building blocks so you will be in a position to receive those blessings. Let's be real, we all know there is a greater force than us present. Why not use that force in our favor? Learn to balance thought and emotion. When you think good thoughts, they spill over to create good emotions, and vice versa. This is what makes the rich richer.

****NOTE: THE MORE CONSCIOUS YOU ARE OF OPPORTUNITIES, THE MORE LIKELY YOU ARE TO WIN. YOU RARELY HEAR PEOPLE SPEAKING OF OPPORTUNITIES AND NOT BENEFITING FROM THEM. OPPORTUNITIES ARE PRESENTED TO ALL THOUGH THEY ARE TAKEN ADVANTAGE OF BY THOSE WHO ARE MOST LIKELY PREPARED! TIME TO PUT YOUR 20/10 HUSTLER VISION TO USE AND MAKE THOSE OPPORTUNITIES WORK FOR *YOU.*

Chapter 5

MORALITY

" **A** rich man once had a conversation with a poor man, and realized just how poor he was."

A genuine hustler will do anything to advance, but not everything. Hustling with a sense of morals is the key to building and maintaining a long and prosperous relationship with inhabitants in your field. Not only does it keep your name in good standing, but it upholds mutual fairness, respect, trust, and agreement between you and those you interact with. The hustler knows fair exchange is never a robbery.

BAD BUSINESS

"I'm still living
I ain't hiding,
I'm riding;
Mac on the side,
Do you really wanna die;
So tell yo shooters bring that money back;
Matter fact-
Once done they can run with that;
I'm generous I'll bury them with it,
'Cause they never should've committed to hitting a killa!"
      — I AIN'T SCARED

I was propositioned to purchase a state-of-the-art building for sale for a music studio. Its owner's shady business reputation preceded him. I was skeptical about dealing with him, but an associate of mine vouched for him. I placed a $20,000 down payment. The Necessary paperwork to secure the building wasn't procured for signatures. Locks were still on the building doors; scheduled meetings were canceled; unanswered calls. This resulted in my confronting the voucher, my associate. After months passed, and pressure applied, this shady property owner paid me back in full.

WIN TOGETHER

"Been getting to it everyday on the block,
Told the plug to send me everything they got;
Cause I gotta feed my team-
Cause we got bigger dreams than the street!"
— ONE OPTION

A friend and I partnered on an investment. In truth, it did not pan out as expected, although other investments I made had.

My friend and I met in the Golden State at a health food restaurant to discuss other business projects. Having a good time reminiscing, sharing individual projects, and showing off our luxury vehicles to one another, it almost slipped my mind to return his previous investment proceeds. Not that I had to give him a cut. He said with surprise, "What's this for? I thought we lost out on that deal?" I replied, "When I win, we all win." "Damn! Appreciate it bro, he said. He'd forgotten all about it. I hadn't.

STRAIGHT TALK

Throughout my years of hustling, I have found that leading with gratitude keeps me on the straight and narrow in all aspects of life. Including Personal, business, and all relationships. In reality, who wants to associate with anyone who is morally incompetent? Or someone who doesn't give a fuck about anything or anyone.

I used to have friends that would say fuck everyone else except for me. For some time, I thought this was loyalty. I had mistaken their ability to fuck over others but show me love as honor and respect. Although beneficial for me, it showed a lack of moral compass on my part.

I learned that how you do one thing is reflected in how you do all things.

I was a bit hypocritical in a sense. A hustler who does good business runs with and or supports friends, family, or teammates. While one who does bad business will ultimately find the prospects of success nil. In essence, you must live by example, or you may find Bullets full of revenge spray in all directions. These are definite deal breakers and will quickly have you blackballed in any industry. My thoughts once were, "They may fuck over them, but they know better than to try it with me." It was a flawed way of thinking. Many hustlers think this way. When people bring up BS or include me in something that is against my morals and principles, I vehemently express my dislike and distaste for the conversation or situation. In fact, do not even bring up no snake shit or bad business vibes to me. Don't even ask my opinion on low vibrational, unproductive conversations. I shut it down. I understand how universal law works. The very company you keep mirrors your mentality. It also plays a major factor in the energy that you attract to yourself. Your vibe attracts your tribe. Guilty by association as to speak. My best advice is to align yourself with people who align with your purpose. If you entertain or take part in negativity, it's contagious and can infect your mind. Pay attention to the people whom you know that are morally void. You will notice the similarities in their thinking and character traits. The number one leading trait besides being a slick/sly/sneaky/slimeball piece of shit is that they think and move with desperation. Moving in haste as if they are in fear of missing out on something. They operate from a level of scarcity, not abundance.

As a true hustler, your morals and principles have to be your foundation. This is what you stand on. What you're willing to live for and die for. Never replace your morals for any amount of money. No dollar amount can make me compromise my morals. I can't be bought. Whether it be your personal life or business affairs, make sure your morals are at the forefront. Once you are morally sound, this will act as a force field to shield you from anything or anyone that is opposite of doing right or righteous hustling.

BAG IT UP/WRAPPING UP A DEAL

Morals are the glue that holds together any lasting relationships and seals most deals. A hustler with a moral compass hardly ever loses business partners or sight of the hustle's goal. You will move with a sense of purpose based on common decency and fairness. It is your token of credibility where your reputation for conducting good business will precede you. A hustler will always be respected for having business morals. You'll amass loyal customers and business associates. Morals are the platform of prosperity. You're sure to gain a reputable name and fortune with moral conduct.

Morals will also navigate you through your competitive, ruthless, and self-centered nature. Without it as your guide, competition will appear as the enemy, and winning will become more important than the mission. Success or achievement is not about winning or losing; it is about having heart and performing at greater levels. Without morals, a ruthless approach amounts only to brutality. With morals, we can be ruthless about our children getting a proper education. Ruthless in support of team members; ruthless about balancing our health and our hustle.

Having Morals takes the "me, me, me" out of your vocabulary and turns it upside down to "we." There are many things more valuable than money: For example: family, life experience, generosity, and good deeds. It's a hustler's pension plan.

MOVING FORWARD

Morality stops the BS. It's the difference between longevity versus being short-lived. One thing about a true hustler is that they know when they aren't playing by the rules. Even buzzard hustlers/con men find it hard to live with themselves after shady deals. They may act as if nothing fazes them, but in reality, when they look at themselves in the mirror, they see the truth. Note that I put emphasis on true hustlers. If you are not true, then you are fake. It's only so long the fake can pretend before it catches up to them. Who doesn't want to do good business? Even scumbags hate getting the short end of the stick. If every choice were to walk away clean, I'm sure that would be the first choice. Think longevity. Think about keeping your name in good standing. Don't get me wrong, I understand that things happen that are sometimes out of a hustler's control. That is why having an understanding is the best thing you can have. When you display morals, people will help keep your name amongst the gods.

****NOTE: YOUR MORALS WILL KEEP YOU WITH THE RIGHT PEOPLE IN THE RIGHT ROOMS. TYPICALLY, PEOPLE WHO DO GOOD BUSINESS ALIGN WITH OTHER PEOPLE WHO DO GOOD BUSINESS. THE GOAL

IS TO DO CONTINUED GOOD, CLEAN BUSINESS, AND GET FAR AWAY FROM THOSE WHO DON'T! YOU NEVER WANT TO GET CAUGHT UP IN SHADY BUSINESS DIRECTLY OR BY ASSOCIATION. IF YOU ARE WITH THEM, THEN YOU'RE JUST AS GUILTY AS THEM.

Chapter 6

Self-Confidence

"**F**inish how you start — Can't come in as a lion but leave as a pussycat."

Before a hustler can have self-confidence, you must first embrace self-belief. As a hustler, if you don't believe in yourself, how can anyone else believe in you? Or believe in any of your ideas, plans or whatever you propose for advancement. When a hustler has selfbelief, it empowers him to make major moves with efficiency and build self-confidence. With confidence, you will know who you are, your strengths and weaknesses, your ability to perform, and assurance to make the right judgment calls.

STAY READY

"They trapped my body
Couldn't trap my mind;
How I'm free,
But still stuck in the grind;
'Cause I was tryna make this hard shit easy,
Walked on water and made this hard shit easy!"

— EASY

My business partners invited me to an NFL player's motivation seminar as a guest. My friends, who are well-educated and great orators, had the audience fully engaged. Though I was there to support them, I became connected with how invested the players were in their speeches. My friends had caught me by surprise when they asked me to speak. I stood up, cleared my throat, and spoke about my experiences, encouraging and inspiring my audience.

STRAIGHT TALK

We must be very careful with self-belief. Insecurities can create and drive a false belief in us all. It's actually what's currently going on in the world of social media, bleeding into our real lives. Example: So many people have created an image on social media that is being supported by likes that the person deems this to be true. As if the person has conned themselves into believing they are the false image with whom they've created. This is dangerous.

Believing in yourself and believing what you are capable of must truly be defined and supported by facts, not merely faith. If you are good at sales, the numbers should reflect that. That is the proof. You gotta bring the receipts. Just saying and thinking or believing you are good at sales only builds morale for your hustle. The confirmation lies in the execution. My advice is not to hype you up on false beliefs but to stand on what you know you can do. Not just what you believe you can do. Take a look at society. Many people think they can do anything just because they see other people doing it. Until they actually attempt it, that is. So please believe in yourself and your ability to accomplish whatever you put your mind to. A hustler knows to base his belief in his ability on probability. He knows the likelihood of his chances of making it happen.

Delusion is anti-hustle.

BAG IT UP

Before a hustler can rely on self-confidence, you must first believe in yourself; in your ability to complete a mission and achieve your goals; belief that you can do and carry out anything. Self-belief is powerful because you judge your own abilities, strengths, and weaknesses. Finding your capabilities for success increases your chances of actual success. What you believe pushes your performance, and how well you perform decides your achievement. When you develop trust in yourself and your abilities, that positive attitude exudes confidence in your skills. Everyone becomes intoxicated by it. Because you have overcome weaknesses: rising to new challenges outside of your comfort zone; speaking at seminars or public assemblies; connecting with others in your environment; and never bowing down to failure. Always try. Self-confidence is having a never-say-die attitude! You know you can do it; make it happen.

MOVING FORWARD

Self-belief/Confidence is the core/backbone of the hustler. This is how seeds get planted —by believing you are who you say you are. Belief builds confidence. Your confidence is a by-product of your belief in yourself. Allow your confidence to bring the trophy to you instead of chasing the win. Believe in yourself 1000% and never let anyone or anything shake that. Once you reach this status, you can simplify your hustle. Remember: you would not be in the position if you could not handle it. So, embrace it, believe in you, and make light work of the task.

****NOTE: SELF-BELIEF IS ONE THING. BUT YOUR CONFIDENCE IS THE ABILITY TO GET THINGS DONE! YOUR ABILITY TO DO A CERTAIN THING WITH CONFIDENCE, MEANS YOU KNOW WHAT YOU'RE DOING! CONFIDENCE STAMPS YOUR EX-PERTISE. PEOPLE CAN BELIEVE THAT THEY CAN DO WHATEVER THEY SET THEIR MIND TOO AND STILL FAIL. CONFIDENCE STARTS WITH SELF-BE-LIEF. YOU MUST BE VERY CRITICAL WITH YOUR JUDGMENT OF THE PEOPLE, PLACES, AND THINGS THAT YOU ATTACH TO YOUR HUSTLE. EVERY FAILURE IS A STRIKING BLOW TO A HUSTLER'S CONFIDENCE. TO BE CONFIDENT IS TO HAVE NO

SECOND GUESSING. TO SAY, "I'M CONFIDENT THAT I CAN WIN" IMPLIES THAT YOU HAVE THIS IN THE BAG. ONE CAN ONLY BE CONFIDENT ABOUT SOMETHING THEY'RE 1000% SURE OF. SO NEVER FOOL YOURSELF INTO BELIEVING YOU'RE CONFIDENT ABOUT SOMETHING THAT YOU'RE NOT. LEARN THE DIFFERENCE AND NEVER CONFUSE THE TWO.

Chapter 7

CLARITY

"**I**n order to shoot your shot, one must have a target."

A hustler who sees the components or elements of their environment executes the hustle without hesitation or corrections. Oftentimes, rework will prove costly to a hustler: time, money, reliability, and a hustler's word or promise to deliver are at stake. The hustle is a hustler's livelihood; you cannot afford to lose it. Learn every aspect of your hustle and you will see things in slow motion and make exact moves necessary to advance and prosper.

BOSS TO CEO

"Talk keys please no ounces
Bosses do boss shit;
Talking 'bout murder,
Detroit that don't cost shit;
On my ceo shit,
Ownership means we don't owe shit;
When I think of views I think oceans!"
  — PROTECTING MY INVESTMENT

An associate had brokered a marijuana deal with some guys to buy 50 lbs. During the meeting, the buyer asked my friend if we could supply another 100 or 200 lbs. His persistence of if we could get more made me paranoid. I had to take control of the deal from my associate and aborted the mission. My associate called me later wanting to resume the deal on his own; reinforcing that these guys were legit. He ended up getting robbed by them.

(INSPIRATION)

I was at a music industry party in Atlanta in 2006. As a new artist, a magazine at the time wanted to interview me.

While driving through Atlanta, I noticed a billboard. It was different from the ordinary Tobacco billboards; it captured the urban experience. Something about it intrigued me then it clicked: I can have billboards in my hometown. At this time, no hip-hop artists had ever promoted themselves or independent labels on billboards, let alone a hustler from Detroit. I knew it was a great way to advertise my record label. "D.W.I." Deal Witt It records.

(BILLBOARDS)

As soon as I got back to Detroit, I made calls until I came in contact with someone at the CBS Outdoor Office. A sales rep there quoted unreasonable prices. Later, I went to the office to meet with the vice president. I built a rapport with him. He respected my ambition and offered me an opportunity to occupy major billboard slots that were vacant at certain times. The deal entailed 50 billboards, 100 buses all over the city, plus kiosks in malls. I marketed my record label's slogan: "WE THE TICKET OUT THE HOOD." The billboards presented my record label as I saw it, epic; bigger than myself, as a recording artist. It catapulted my record label, Deal Witt It (DWI) to the general public.

FUTURE

"I just want family to look up to me
That mean you special if you close to me;
Told her baby just believe in me,
Sometimes I don't know what you see in me;
I trust in G.O.D.!"

— WIN

I was introduced to a young talented college student, who was an upcoming producer in the industry. His beats were soulful and hard-hitting. We began working together. I purchased beats from him anytime he had something hot. He was young, ambitious, and on the come up. He would comment on my lifestyle, showing growing interest. He was more than aware of my line of business. One day he mentioned that he and his friend could sell a lot of marijuana on campus. I gave him a keyboard instead. He went on to be one of the top producers/songwriters in the game.

STRAIGHT TALK

You have to be able to see clearly and think clearly to clear checks. A clear mind will be most valuable to a hustler. You can't have your mind clouded by any drama. Whether it be from a relationship or on the job. There's no room for it where you're headed. This is a first-class flight, with you and motivation. We used to have a saying, "The bullshit can take a backseat." But scratch that, I don't even want it in the car with me. Stay focused. Full speed ahead. Distractions will constantly present themselves. Your hustle depends on you to be so focused that you see the distractions from a mile away. It's been times when I couldn't even entertain my family issues. I was on a mission to accomplish a goal. Understand that whatever is going on will be there when you get back. Having the capability to solve problems takes clarity. Being able to see the puzzle in its entirety, so you can eye the pieces that actually fit. We are all here to win something. For some, it may be love, money, respect, accolades, etc. All of them sound good to me. I'm sure you agree. With that being said, use clarity to position yourself to win. Never choose shooting a three-pointer over making a layup. Give me the sure easy two. Unless I need a three to win the game.

BAG IT UP

A hustler recognizes the rules and customs in their environment. By acknowledging all the elements and roles on any given playing field, you will know what positions are available and which you will assume. Study your surroundings and its inhabitants. It is proven that taught behavior is reactionary, inside-the-box thinking. Whereas, studying transcends to intuitive or gut feeling, on the side of precaution. Then you will be able to see moves and make moves in advance; and put necessary components together for major projects. And, you won't hardly ever have to repeat a task or mission; you'll reach your objectives the first time.

MOVING FORWARD

Clarity is the chess player in you. Being able to tap into that hustler's vision to see moves ahead. This places you at an advantage over the johnny-come-lately or the late bloomers who think they are steps ahead of the rest. This makes all the difference in the world in advancement. Apply this in every aspect of your life. Whether family, friends, relationships, or business, don't just listen to the story; see it from all sides. This will give you the edge to practice discernment in all situations. There is no one way to look at a thing; even when it appears to be clear-cut. A hustler must never rule out the obvious.

Remember, as a hustler you are digging for gold. And that requires a lot of mental digging and sifting through tons of dirt. Whatever you start/begin you must already see a glimpse of the finish/end. Once done correctly, people will see this as a gift.

Like a psychic ability. That's that hustler's vision.

****NOTE: ANOTHER IMPORTANT ROLE CLARITY PLAYS IN A HUSTLER'S LIFE IS TRANSPARENCY! THIS REQUIRES A CERTAIN LEVEL OF COMMUNICATION TO MAKE SURE THAT EVERYONE IS ON THE SAME PAGE AND FULLY UNDERSTANDS WHAT'S AT STAKE. MAKE SURE YOU GO OVER THE MISSION AS MANY TIMES AS NEEDED. YOU MAY SOUND CRAZY OR LIKE A BROKEN RECORD. AT LEAST NO ONE WILL BE ABLE TO MAKE ANY EXCUSES. TOTAL TRANSPARENCY IS NECESSARY SO THAT ALL PARTIES ARE FULLY AWARE OF WHAT THEY ARE AGREEING TO. FOR THIS REASON, CLARITY CAN'T BE STRESSED ENOUGH!

IT AIN'T NO FUTURE IN YOUR FRONTIN'

Another level of transparency in the hustle is knowing when to expose your hand. From the streets to the infamous Hollywood saying, "fake it til you make it" is prevalent. Especially in this social media era. Which works in some instances, but I can't front. No pun intended.

On the flip side, I've seen being transparent work just the same. Even better in certain instances. Let's break it down: acting like you have it together is just that, an act. Many fall for it. Some don't. The only thing about frontin/acting is that it's not really who you are, not really what you know, or not really what you can do. This poses a threat to you potentially being exposed. "It ain't no future in your frontin." Bullshit can get you to the top, but it will not keep you there. Bullshitting is short-lived. There's no longevity in not being who you truly are.

Also, there is a deep level of fear rooted in trying to keep up whatever image you subscribed to. In the hood, we call it keeping your fronts up. It is a known fact that no one wants to deal with someone who does not have their shit together. If we look around us, we will see most people in this world are hiding from themselves. No one can truly be themselves. From the drug dealer to the president. The way things are set up, no one can even have an opinion more the less voice their opinion. Fear of getting stoned to non-existence by "cancel culture". Or judged by or made fun of by your peers. So, everyone portrays an image. Whether at the job, home, church, club, etc., It's a lifestyle and the norm nowadays.

A hustler is only as good as his last hustle. So, when he chooses to operate from a finesse standpoint, he becomes a buzzard hustler /conman. When you are finessing to get what you want. Regardless of how far that gets you, it will not last long. Due to the other party being played or ripped off, word will quickly spread. It's super easy to tarnish your name, and almost impossible to get your name back in good standing. At the end of the day, money will come and go, status will come and go, and even people will come and go. THOUGH YOUR NAME SHOULD LIVE FOREVER!!

There are some exceptions to the rule when playing the role to get on: Acting! Some actors get the part. Now I've seen individuals with good intentions make it like this. When your intentions are good, they weed out the smoke and mirrors. How many times have you done something to impress some-one? Whether it was a potential business or someone you were interested in dating, we all are guilty of doing things to win others over. There's nothing wrong with this, as long as your intentions are pure. The truth will take precedence and shine through.

There is another side to where fronting can go wrong. When a hustler needs assistance or help. Whether it be needing a recommendation, help financially, or a walk through the door. When you are guarding your image with your life... that's what it can cost you. This creates a certain level of stubbornness which hinders a hustler and becomes self-sabotaging. You can kill your dream and all that you have worked hard for due to a hustler's ego/ false pride. It will prevent you from asking for help or assistance from anyone. It is likened to a hustler drowning on a sinking boat. I've been guilty of this on many occasions. Even while I'm writing this, I had to remind myself to ask for help for a business venture I'm working on. The problem is that asking for help puts you in a vulnerable position, giving someone else control. Where they can either say yes or no. But closed mouths don't get fed. No one can do it by themselves. Look at any of the greats: entrepreneurs, icons, to thought leaders. Teams win championships. Not one person.

Vulnerability is not a weakness. It is actually a strength. It's showing a side of you that is your true self.

My brand/lifestyle "Health-n-Hustle" allows me to be my true self. Not just the image of the gangster rapper known as

"Detroit King Tape". Learn the difference between what image you're portraying. Distinguishing the two will help you act, plus respond accordingly.

The goal for everyone should be to grow and change for the better. Evolution is inevitable. A hustler is in control of what he becomes.

Chapter 8

Ownership

"**E**verything outside of you is leased — unless you, too, are living outside of yourself."

Owning your hustle. It's achieved by knowing yourself, your environment, and having an unobstructed vision of your objectives. By not owning your hustle, you allow others to take control of it and therefore, take control of you.

STEP UP

"Detroit is in the building,
Detroit is in the building;
Naw we never left man-
We was just chilling;
Now we back-
We what the industry missing!"

— MOTOWN

I went from owning drug houses to owning state-of-the-art recording studios throughout the city of Detroit. The most notable studio I owned was 1250 Griswold St. in Downtown Detroit. I renovated a 12,000 square foot old bank. I invested over a few hundred thousand in bringing the studio to life. Many major artists from Detroit recorded notable hits there. A topnotch studio represented my lifestyle, career, and legacy. That's why I went above and beyond in renovation. I was pulling permits, refacing the building, and upgrading everything inside. I brought so much attention to myself that my lawyer contacted me. He said, "You need to slow down, you're a street guy -— convicted felon, spending hundreds of thousands, in the downtown of a major city." People were watching. I named it Industry Sound Studio. I envisioned making Detroit a major center for hip-hop music at a time when the music industry was shunning the city. Today, the light shines on the Detroit music scene and Detroit artists.

INSPIRED

"Can't sell dope forever-
Get yo business up;
Crib too small for a baller,
Get yo ceilings up;
Don't love nothing you can't leave-
Get yo feelings crushed;
Living by the heat,
30 seconds flat I'm packing up!"

— BALLING

Ups and downs, going back to the drawing board. I found digging deep within lies truth and an answer; that my life was unbalanced; that my health strengthened my hustle; and that I could draw strength from my diet and energize my ability to refrain from eating unhealthy. I realized if I don't control what I put into my body, how can I control anything in my life? It's when it hit me — Health N hustle isn't just a brand, but a way of life. I have created an outlet for myself that can also motivate and inspire others.

STRAIGHT TALK

What you own belongs to you. No one should be able to stake a claim or take it away from you. Thus, the reason we have titles, deeds, receipts, etc. This also applies to your hustle. It's quite easy to show you own something tangible. Now let me show you how this translates to the hustle. A hustle in a nutshell is a perfected trade. The majority of hustlers do not have degrees. What they have learned cannot be defined by a certificate or a piece of paper. Hustlers take the basic knowledge of a trade and put their sauce on it to make it work the way they see fit. You have to use tact to create your own style to maintain high performance in your own lane. Sure, a hustle can be taught. A person can pick up on a thing or two about the hustle. How to move a product a certain way or how to provide a service in an eloquent manner. Though to perform with continuous precision can't be taught. The drive must be in you. You cannot teach drive. However, if you have an inkling of drive in you; you can acquire the rest.

We're presently in the era of the largest creative space ever. Every time I pick up my phone, I see another creator or creative idea winning. All from their hustle. A million people can do the same thing. Though each person will have a special way they do it. The way they talk, walk, rap, act, deliver, perform, cook, dance, etc. Pay attention to how these creators own their hustle. See what special niche you can offer to yours, and go out and own your hustle.

BAG IT UP

The hustle is like reality, it belongs to no one; it's only what you make of it. What you create out of the ether is your possession. Your hustle is formed and shaped in the same way as your life — forged out of the earth's elements as is your individuality. It's imperative that you own your hustle as you do your life. Take ownership of the distinct manner in which you operate your business; ethics and principles; character (the type of person you really are — no apologies); your words, actions, and deeds. As with life, all these aspects are incorporated into your hustle. Be conscious that responsibility comes with ownership. The more you own, the greater the responsibility. If you do not take possession of it, others will. Where the very thing you made is taken away from you out of irresponsibility, that's to say, because you did not have a sense of ownership to begin with. See that it's really your world and everything in it. Own it!

MOVING FORWARD

Ownership in layman's terms is "Own your shit." Take pride in what you are good at. You should be passionate about what you are good at. That's how you perfect your trade. This gives you the ability to take your hustle to the next level. Understand that a hustle is nothing more than a perfected trade. Where You become so great at doing a thing that you make it look easy. If you are good at stacking cups, embrace that trade and learn how to turn it into a hustle. Create a course on how to stack cups etc. I'm sure you get the gist. Whatever you do, just never half ass anything. If you commit to something, give it your best. Your hustler's reputation depends on the quality of work and efficiency of how well you execute. Never downplay what you commit to. Oh, I was just doing that just to get through or get by. Never do or say this. This is self-sabotaging. Because that small job or act could be judged by a bigger job. If you commit to it, see it through with a hustler's excellence. In the same regard, never commit to what does not serve your interest. A hustler gravitates towards things that inspire his/her creativity. Anything else will be forced and poorly executed.

****NOTE: OWNERSHIP DOESN'T HAVE TO AP-PLY TO ALL BUSINESS VENTURES. SOME SUCCESS-FUL BUSINESSES ARE RUN OFF OPERATING AGREE-MENTS BY OWNERS/PARTNERS. SO, WHEN WE SPEAK OF OWNERSHIP, IT'S MORE GEARED TO-WARD YOU PLANTING YOUR FLAG AND CLAIM-ING YOUR TERRITORY. THIS FIRST STARTS IN YOUR MIND. BEING THAT MOST PEOPLE DON'T HAVE CONTROL OVER THEIR LIVES, BECAUSE THEY DON'T OWN THEIR THOUGHTS. IT'S IM-PORTANT TO KNOW THAT THE THOUGHT IS THE CAUSE OF IT ALL. SO HAVING CONTROL OF YOUR MIND, GIVES YOU CONTROL OF YOUR CRE-ATIVE THOUGHTS. THIS IS A LIFELONG MEDITA-TIVE PROCESS. ONCE IN ALIGNMENT, A HUSTLER WILL FUNCTION WITH PRECISION.

Chapter 9

MASTERY

I t takes 10,000 hours to achieve your master's degree —
and a split second to lose it all."

A hustler's calling is to acquire self-actualization. It is the full realization of your intelligence, creativity, and social influence. It's also awareness of your abilities and limitations, such as your mind working against your goals if you are not in control of your emotions. Mastery can be a talent or skill that anyone can acquire through study and discipline. You will know that all things are possible, as it only takes will and drive. You will see that your projection of success is in everyone and everything that you touch. Comprehending every angle of your hustle and putting it into practice is mastery.

ASCENDANCE

"I'm tryna please everybody and keep them happy
but I'm spreading myself thin;
Trying not to let the devil in!"

— WIN

I recently had a production deal where I stood to make $10k from connecting some entertainment friends together. I was totally fine with my share. After the deal was completed, I realized that through my leverage I could have made up to $50k instead. It was not the money left on the table so much as undermining myself as an indispensable asset. I kicked myself in the ass. I promised myself afterward to always look ahead or live a life of regrets.

STRAIGHT TALK

Your goals materialize when all elements within your being are functioning properly and in harmony. Do you ever recall times when it seems like everything is lining up perfectly, or everything is working in your favor? It may be luck for some people, though with a hustler's mentality, it is less luck and more manifestation for those who practice alignment and balance. Winners attract wins. Take two magnets. They have two ends: north and south poles. When they are lined up in sequence they attract. However, once they face one another they repel. Same as if cars tailing each other in the same lane can cover miles. But turn one of those cars around and it's a head-on collision. This is indicative of how the mind, body, and universe work. Focus on getting these three in alignment and your world will change. Do activities that balance the mind, spirit, and body daily. If you are too stressed; you run away from the check. The lack of gratitude limits your aptitude. And so on. You get the gist. Mastery is an accumulation of balanced components. Never seek out mastery. For you will never luck up on it. It is better to work on balancing all areas of your life to stay in harmony with the universal frequencies, to which you gravitate.

BAG IT UP

To understand your environment and its elements in such a way as to manipulate power moves comes from ascension. Never depreciate your skills; least of all out of modesty or sparing of other's feelings. Some are born with the talent of mastery; others must develop it. Either case, it's an aptitude for deeper understanding and greater achievements. At some point in your life, you realized your potential and brought it to fruition, a leader in life, trade, and social skills. Who you are is undeniable. What you do is exceptional. You are a hustler, a master of your hustle.

MOVING FORWARD

Trace your steps to see how you could have added more value or done it better. Take the time to reflect on your win-to-win easier next time. The victory is never over. Life is ever evolving. Our knowledge, our information must be continually upgraded in order to stay ahead of the game. Being current isn't good enough. A hustler must stay ahead of the curve. A hustler's saying," True game is not something you can peep out while a person is running it on you. True game is when you make it home and realize that a person just got over on you." Whether it be getting you out of time, energy, money, etc.

Mastery is such an important plus pivotal part of a hustler's advantage and advancement. A leader's sole position is to simplify things so all components can function at a level of excellence and perfect symmetry. To do something great is an achievement. Though to continually do great things is awesome. To remain on top is far harder than becoming a onetime champion. Defending the title requires more work than it takes to just win the title. A sucker can luck up. The sun shines on a dog's ass every now and then. Though to hear those words, "and still the champion," requires a certain level of knowing your environment, overcoming the fear, and turning that fear into that hustler's aggression. That opens the door of opportunity to morally support the self-belief in you. Which in turn builds the confidence that creates the clarity for the hustler to stand on what he says. Plus own everything that he attaches himself to. Reaching a level of mastery once all codes are incorporated is a daily practice for the hustler. The more you learn, and apply these codes, the easier the execution becomes. You will have seen it all before. You will visualize things in your head before they play out in your life. I once zoned out in a studio session during a freestyle; it was as if I was in a time warp. As if the beat slowed down, I visually saw each word as I took and placed them in the perfect spot. This was the best freestyle session ever for me. I knew then what was possible.

Self-mastery is equivalent to becoming a great chess player. Knowing life may respond like that if you move like this... I always applied the "planting the seed method." Especially in relationships. Isn't that what life's all about (relationships) no matter who it is, or what title? Every human interaction has the potential to develop into a relationship. Therefore, you need to plant seeds. Make sure to extend your hand/courtesy to relationships that you look forward to building. Learn how to nurture the relationship. This will by far be the most effective tool of the hustle codes. Relationships open the doors, that millions of dollars can't. Remember this. And take note of this:

Whenever I'm introduced to someone who could potentially add value to me or vice versa. I like to think about what potential moves can be made on the board of life. It can be as simple as getting extra napkins/utensils because you know everyone will need them, or offering a seat that is more suitable to the guest especially if they're visiting. The smallest accommodations/gestures show your consideration. And people who value relationships take notice of this.

I was once invited to a friend's photo shoot. I made sure he had water, behind-the-scenes footage, etc. This wasn't my job, but I saw it was a need, so I accommodated him. Never allow your pride to stop you from being a key piece of the puzzle. Remember a strong leader quality is to simplify a task. So that everything can flow smoothly. On many occasions this has opened doors, garnering great opportunities for me. Never feel some type of way about being a boss but playing the role of the door attendant. I have unintentionally left so many great impressions that people talk about how helpful I was when I was not around. What they say about you when you leave the room is what counts. I would get calls/invites or just plain interest or good comments from people who met me through friends. They would say things like —

"I like Tape."
"He's alright."
"He has great energy."
"He's down to earth."

In reality, I was unconsciously planting the seeds for our

next encounter or meeting. Whereas everyone would be more welcoming. Show them that you're willing to be a team player and do whatever it takes. Learning to treat others how you would like to be treated is mastery.

****NOTE: MASTERY ALSO COMES FROM A GENUINE PLACE OF GRATITUDE. RECOGNIZING THAT YOU HAVE EVOLVED AND MATURED IN AN ECOSYSTEM WHERE ITS "DOG EAT DOG"!

REMEMBER THAT MASTERY HAS MORAL OBLIGATIONS. TO RESPECT LIFE IN ALL WALKS OF LIFE. RESPECT THE LIFESTYLES AND OPINIONS OF OTHERS. AS A HUSTLER, THESE CODES PROMOTE INDEPENDENCE AND INDIVIDUALITY.

MY FAVORITE SLOGAN, "RESPONSIBILITY COMES WITH BEING REAL". YOU HAVE TO STAND IN YOUR TRUTH! STAND ON BUSINESS! DON'T JUST CLAIM A TITLE, OWN WHOMEVER YOU ARE. AT THIS STAGE, PEOPLE SHOULD KNOW EXACTLY WHAT THEY'RE GETTING IF THEY RING YOUR PHONE. EVERYTHING YOU DO SHOULD REPRESENT EXACTLY WHO YOU ARE AS A PERSON AND A HUSTLER. ALL OF YOUR WORKING COMPONENTS MUST MESH WELL TOGETHER SO AS TO SHOW CONSISTENT THINKING, BELIEF, AND MOVEMENT.

EVERY MOVING PART SHOULD FUNCTION PLUS VIBRATE AT A CERTAIN CAPACITY. WE ARE ALL

ONE PART OF THE WHOLE. EQUAL IS THE HUMAN RACE. EQUAL IS ALL LIVING SPECIES. LIFE IS TRULY FOR THE LIVING. MAKE SURE YOUR PHILOSOPHY IS SYNONYMOUS WITH HELPING LIFE EVOLVE. DO YOUR PART. YOUR CONTRIBUTION STARTS WITH YOU. THEN SHARE WITH THE WORLD.

Chapter 10

CONSIGLIERE

"The sun never concerns itself with how bright it gets —its rays are the proof."

After mastering your hustle, you are in a position to elevate others to tap into their inner hustler. Lend your expertise, especially to those you discern can use it for the betterment of their lives and surroundings so that they may take the opportunity and gain ownership of their lives; that it may spread and inspire others to change their environment to a fair playing field for all hustlers. Gain personal satisfaction in knowing the hustle has been preserved.

SHALOM

"That's why we gotta keep balling,
Let no man stop us;
Or come between us making millions of dollars;
Told my momma yea I love you-
And I'm tryna make it for us;
They got it loaded for me
I'm just tryna make it to it;
I gotta keep balling-
Making these flips;
I always knew that I would do it this big;
told my brother man let's get it—
Told my team we gon make it-
Told my plug all the dirt that we did I keep it sacred!"

— BALLING

I recently had a meeting with my partners in our Ceen-verde tequila brand. We were laughing about guys in our neighborhood back in Detroit. They were telling one of my partners that they saw him hanging with the guy who was on all that motivational shit [me., "Detroit King Tape"]. They were saying it in an acknowledgment with respect... As we laughed and toasted to our future tequila endeavors, I told them, "My plan is working." As my goal was to reinvent myself.

****NOTE: THIS IS SOMETHING WE ALL HAVE TO CONTINUALLY DO AS HUSTLERS. SEEING HOW THE HUSTLE IS EVER EVOLVING AND HOW SHORT THE ATTENTION SPAN OF THE MASSES IS WITH ALL OF THE SOCIAL MEDIA TRAINING OUR MINDS TO VIEW EVERYTHING IN A MINUTE'S CAPACITY. BEING KNOWN AS A GANGSTER/GANGSTA RAPPER FOR YEARS. IT'S A RELIEF TO BE ABLE TO BE KNOWN FOR MOTIVATING AND INSPIRING PEOPLE TO BETTER THEMSELVES IN EVERY ASPECT VERSUS JUST PROMOTING VIOLENCE AND GETTING MONEY. THERE COMES A POINT IN LIFE WHEN THE MESSENGER HAS TO EVALUATE THE MESSAGE HE/SHE IS SENDING.

In the state of hip hop where a mother raps about derogatory/degrading content, (i.e., Fuck him, then get his money. Pussy ain't free, etc.) Sure, she has an epiphany and turns that shit off! When her young daughter starts singing along. This is the sign of the hustle code morality actually hitting home. I can relate, listening to some of my music has had a similar effect on me. Since shifting my environment mentally and physically, I no longer think or live in the conditions I did before. Nor do I partake in or see most of the things I once did. Therefore, the bars in my songs are a little different. What was once a reality rap for me is now a reflection of how I used to live. Chapter 2: Fear breaks down how I once allowed the fear of my environment to fuel thoughts of being killed or getting sentenced to life in prison for committing crimes. Which resulted in the following bars:

I HEAR THESE NIGGAS WANNA KILL ME;
WELL TELL 'EM I AIN'T SCARED
I'M LIVIN I AIN'T DEAD"

— I AIN'T SCARED

I was rolling the dice with my life. I really was transporting, smuggling, and selling drugs that could have landed me in prison with a life sentence. I am one of the blessed ones who has lived to talk about it. I've served my prison time, a total of 10 years out of my life. I'm fortunate to say that life has been behind me for years now. Coming from being motivated to sell a kilo of drugs, to being inspired & motivated to inspire others, by sharing my story. This is an example of morality, opportunism, self-belief/confidence, aggression, and clarity at their finest. Having a moral epiphany made me take accountability to take that opportunity to better myself – having the clarity to see the vision to get out of the game and off the streets. Believing in myself and confirming it with confidence by applying good aggression as the fuel to spread my thoughts, views, and experiences worldwide. People ask me what made me start speaking, and what inspired me to change. My honest assessment is that I always wanted more in life. Despite all the tragedies, losses, friends getting killed, heavy prison sentences, family grief, etc. Despite the downside I was so accustomed to the lifestyle that I enjoyed the life I lived. Knowing that I was a silverback gorilla in the concrete jungle gave me a false sense of kingdom. Not only was I a boss, but being a great leader and a great earner, earned me the name King Tape. And I owned it. The hustler's code, clarity, brought me here as a motivator. I realized that being an O.G. (original gangster) is status, holds respect, and gets you love and salutes. My vision is to flip the term OG (owning growth, officially grown, etc.). We need to redefine the term. And all that that position entails. How does an OG contribute to the youth and his community? There are far too many falsely claiming to be OGs nowadays. Age and survival cannot be the only components of being an OG. But that's another discussion for a future book.

STRAIGHT TALK

There's no better feeling than putting someone up on game, schooling them, or teaching them something. It's an honor to share what you learned when you know it will benefit others and it takes nothing away from you at the same time. It's the saying, "No harm no foul." There is nothing new up under the sun. Only different ways we may say, do, or present something. I learned as a rapper that we all are rapping the same or similar lyrics, though it's how clever you can say it that separates you as an artist. I actually applied this method to other business ventures, and wherever else I could in my everyday life. This is putting your spin on a thing. Adding your twist to it. Or putting your sauce on it. It's the same thing as when cartels put their stamps on their drugs. I learned that they were really just adding their logo. It was a brilliant business strategy. It's actually branding a product. Letting the world know that this is your product. So they know what to expect. There were times when buyers would only cop (purchase) drugs if they had a certain stamp on them.

Even if you had a product that was better quality it didn't matter. They were sold on a certain stamp. It was really a mind game. I found myself losing sales due to this. As a hustler, I had to get creative. I recreated a device that allowed me to repackage the product and put the stamp the buyers were in love with on the product. Hey, can't blame me. Besides, I knew I wasn't going to be taken to court for copyright infringement. I had to give the people what they wanted. That was the past. I took some business strategies that I learned and applied them to legal business ventures. If you can build a name, you can brand a product. Branding a product goes further than just adding a stamp or a logo. It's in the chemistry of the product. It's the difference between eating your mother's home-cooked meal opposed to a stranger's cooking. You are familiar with that taste. Truthfully, it may taste nasty to the majority, though it's what you are used to. Same thing with McDonald's fries. The taste of those fries speaks for itself no matter how unhealthy they are. Learn how to do the same thing with your product or service. Put your sauce on it. Make sure that everything you touch or do reflects something about you. Now that's a bar for a future song.

BAG IT UP

"Each one, teach one," is the intention of true masters. This philosophy of a time-old adage is to not only share the information which you have learned, but also, to preserve the teaching, the tradition, the culture, and the game aka the hustle. A master is never game-conscious or fearful of the next protege or losing control. Instead, a master applies a moral-aggressive approach to teaching what others try to sell or cuff. Masters do not hoard or profiteer the knowledge. They offer it to others so that they can also benefit and change their reality.

MOVING FORWARD

The application of what a hustler learned is evident in the execution of his hustle. The passing along of knowledge/information through conversation, action, and or accomplishment. How much do you share what you've learned? Each one, teach one is an idea I had for a nonprofit organization. As a hustler, I know that sharing is a necessity to keep the hustle alive.

2020 was a year for hustlers. It was the Covid 19 lockdown. Which brought out the hustler in everyone. You had to tap into your resources to survive or thrive. As I sat back and watched the BLM protest from my penthouse in Los Angeles. I saw many loopholes to where I profited nicely. This also became a time that I found it easiest to share my story and reinvent myself in the hip-hop/motivator space. I started speaking and posting daily on social media. Building my following as a motivator. I saw a need for information to be shared now more than ever. People needed to hear some real talk after their lives had been shaken up. Four years later, my mission or my statement hasn't changed. Strange thing is that I've always been known as a gangster rapper/drug dealer/ street guy. Though, now people follow me for inspiration and motivation.

A major key to staying sharp and on point is sharing what you've learned. Which in turn strengthens what you know. Every time you share information, you recall and relearn the information until it becomes second nature. Until you have it down pact or to a science, as if it's implanted into your brain.

Practice sharing what you learn on a daily basis. This makes you smarter, all the while teaching others.

I hope you all learned how to tap into your hustler's mindset through these hustle codes. I enjoyed writing and sharing these codes with you all. Be inspired and motivated to inspire and motivate others.

Self-improvement is the movement. I'm out.

ABOUT THE AUTHOR

Detroit King Tape is a man of integrity and a multifaceted talent. As an author, songwriter, rapper, actor, and motivator, he embodies a diverse range of skills and passions. Raised on the East side of Detroit, Michigan, his limited opportunities pushed him to become a beacon of light for many others who mirrored his lifestyle. His slogan, "Perfection isn't real - Balance is," reflects his Health-n-Hustle lifestyle.

Dedicated to all things health and well-being, Detroit King Tape is an avid writer, thinker, hiker, and manifestor. His daily meditation practices focus on calming the mind, and he draws inspiration from studying the many greats who paved the way before him. His tribute to these pioneers is his commitment to helping as many people as he can. Placing good deeds at the forefront of his conversations allows him to be the creative force that he is. Always finding ways to motivate and inspire others, Detroit King Tape remains on a path of enlightenment.